THE BEST MAN'S
DUTIES

Also available as Paperfronts:

SAMPLE SOCIAL SPEECHES
RIGHT JOKE FOR THE RIGHT OCCASION
JOKE AFTER JOKE AFTER JOKE . . .
JOKES FOR TELLING
APT & AMUSING QUOTATIONS
*WEDDING ETIQUETTE PROPERLY EXPLAINED

*By the same author

THE
BEST MAN'S
DUTIES

by

VERNON HEATON

PAPERFRONTS
**ELLIOT RIGHT WAY BOOKS,
KINGSWOOD, SURREY, U.K.**

Printed and bound in Great Britain by Cox & Wyman Ltd., Reading.

CONTENTS

1

Introduction

I wonder how many young men have accepted, on the spot and without thought, the invitation of a very close friend to be the best man at his wedding?

Too many, I fear, will have jumped at the offer with delight, seeing ahead of them the tempting opportunity to pull the leg of a best friend and to become the leader in all the customary pranks that have long been associated with a man's betrothal and wedding. To encourage and assist a coterie of fellow spirits in stuffing the bridegroom's suitcases with confetti in such a manner that when they are opened in the honeymoon hotel, the confetti will burst forth in a cloud to settle all over the bedroom leaving the staff in no doubt as to the purpose of the stay and to spread the word throughout the hotel; to tie a collection of old shoes to the back of the 'going away' car together with a cardboard notice drawing the attention of passers-by to the embarrassed occupants – and to string together a few facetious comments as a speech to be given at the reception, to raise as much laughter as possible at the expense of the newly-weds.

Not many young men will give such an invitation sufficient consideration before agreeing to accept the task – and sober thought is needed as the duties of a best man can hardly be classed as a job for the practical joke department.

In fact the best man will have to understand that he will be expected to act as a master-of-ceremonies, as a chief marshal in charge of movements, a toastmaster, dispenser of oil on troubled waters, paymaster, messenger, persuader, remembrancer, chief liaison officer between the bridegroom and the bridal contingent – and a repository for such valuables as the wedding ring, cash, documents for the honeymoon – and lost property.

To those of you who have, wittingly or unwittingly, agreed to shoulder the responsibilities of escorting a bridegroom to his wedding, I dedicate the following chapters; and to those who have not yet been dragooned into accepting the 'honour' – be warned!

2

Qualifications

The choice of the best man is the sole prerogative of the bridegroom. Not even the bride has the right to interfere – though it is not unknown for her wishes to have influenced a final choice.

A man's best friend is the almost universal selection for the honour – be he brother, more distant relative or perhaps a life-long companion. That is, if he is still unmarried.

Though there is no rule about the matter, it is customary to make the choice from single men.

But it takes all sorts to make a world and though many of the eligible young men may be paragons of all that is likeable, too many of them fail to meet up with the particular attributes best suited for such a specialised occasion.

Before the offer is made, therefore, the bridegroom should give careful consideration to the following facets in the character of his prospective choice:

(a) Is he eager and happy to accept the duty – or is he merely going to do it 'if he has to'?

(b) Has he the ability and the necessary enthusiasm to carry out the detailed task of organising the event – and of dealing with the practical tasks that arise?

(c) Can he make a speech without being a bore?

(d) Is he quick-witted enough to deal with an emergency? Such as when the nervous bridegroom drops the wedding ring; the bride fails to turn up on time; the parson gets his dates mixed up and they arrive to find the church door locked against them?

Is the Best Man quick-witted enough?

Though unlikely, such slip-ups do occur from time to time.

(e) Can he be relied on to safeguard the ring and the other items that will come under his charge? And will he remember where he is keeping them?

Points regarding his status and situation must also be taken into account, such as:

(a) Is he single or married?

(b) Is he sufficiently *persona grata* with the bride and her parents not to cause resentment and ill-feeling between them and the bridegroom and his family – even though the selection is no real concern of the bride?

(c) Is he certain to be available to take part in the ceremony on the date and will he have time to help in the pre-planning and practical arrangements that must be made in advance?

And despite the care with which the bridegroom chooses his best man, he will indeed be fortunate to escape both criticism and resentment – from his relatives, friends and, possibly, the bride.

The chosen escort should give as much thought to the question of accepting the invitation to be best man as the bridegroom has given to his selection. He should know even better than the bridegroom of any impediment that militates against the successful performance of his duties. Perhaps he has not the time at his disposal to give full attention to the event; maybe he feels that the responsibility is too onerous for him – and possibly he just imagines the role too uncomfortable for his liking.

If he should have any doubt about either the propriety or wisdom of accepting the bridegroom's invitation, he should decline at once. The decision must not be left to the last minute, nor should he change his mind at the last minute – leaving the bridegroom with little chance of finding a suitable replacement.

3

The Ushers

As arrangements for the wedding must be made some time in advance of the event, it is necessary for the bridegroom to nominate his best man as soon after the engagement as is possible and convenient.

It does sometimes happen, however, that the chosen best man lives far from the bridegroom and out of touch with day-to-day events. He may be a 'best friend' who is studying or working far away – perhaps even a member of one of the Services and possibly stationed overseas. He may, because of such circumstances, be able to travel to the venue of the wedding and to stay there for but a few days – perhaps for the day of the wedding only.

Yet, despite the difficulties and frustrations involved, it may well be that the bridegroom holds this particular friend or relative in such high esteem that he is unwilling to be escorted to his wedding by anyone else.

The answer to the problem is the appointment of another friend – possibly the 'next best friend' – as chief usher. The choice of such an individual should be made by consultation between the bridegroom and the best man bearing in mind that:

(a) He must be willing, capable and have the time to act as deputy to the best man during probably the whole of the preliminaries.

(b) He must be well known and a friend of the bridegroom as they will be involved together in making the arrangements and of carrying out the practical details.

(c) He must be a close friend of the best man who will expect him to have ready, and be able to turn over to him with the shortest of briefings, all the information and items he will require for the wedding.

It is not necessary to list here the duties of a chief usher – they are, of course, those of a best man, up to and until the best man is available to take over himself.

In consultation with his best man, the bridegroom should appoint the necessary ushers – or 'groomsmen' as they are sometimes called. The number required will depend largely on the scale of the invitations to the church. Two ushers are perhaps within the generally accepted scale where the number of guests are fewer than 50–60. A further two could well be added to cope with each additional 50–60 though there is no hard and fast ruling on the matter. The need is to have sufficient ushers to receive the guests in the church porch and to conduct them to their places for the service.

Besides appointing ushers for their specific duties, the bridegroom and his best man have to take into account family 'considerations'. It is usual to make the choice from the unmarried brothers and friends of both the bridegroom and his bride and a great deal of tact needs to be exercised if somebody is not going to protest: 'If you ask *him*; you can't leave out *so-and-so*'.

It is important however that each side should be represented in order that as many as possible of the guests will be recognised and received by name. It is quite in order for an usher to meet a guest in the porch

The need is to have sufficient ushers ...

and ask, 'Friend of the bride; or of the groom?', in order to determine his or her place in the body of the church, but it is much more welcoming to receive them by name and, therefore, know the pew to which they should be conducted.

The correct seating arrangements are:

Parents, relatives and friends of the *bride* should be seated in the pews on the left of the nave facing the altar.

Parents, relatives and friends of the *bridegroom*

The bride's relatives.

should be seated in the pews on the right of the nave facing the altar.

In each case, parents, grandparents, brothers and sisters should occupy the front pews, leaving enough room for the groom and best man in the front right hand pew, and immediately behind them, other relatives followed by friends.

The ushers should seat themselves near the back in order to be in a convenient position to deal with any late-comers.

4

Duties

Before listing the precise duties of the best man it must be pointed out that he needs to establish close contact and good relations with the chief bridesmaid. This liaison is of very great importance if many of the trying little details are not to be neglected or their neglect leave a tiny spark of irritation to mar, however slightly, the 'day of days'.

In all probability the bride will come from the same circle of friends as her groom – and choose her chief bridesmaid from the same source. In that event it is a foregone conclusion that the best man will have no difficulty in meeting the chief bridesmaid and that any help required by the one or the other, will be readily forthcoming.

It may happen, of course, that the bride is a stranger to the best man – or that she has nominated a chief bridesmaid who is unknown to him. In such an event the bridegroom should set the matter right as soon as possible. In fact it would be well if the bridegroom together with his bride, invited the best man and the chief bridesmaid to an outing with them – as soon as possible after the announcement of the engagement. A small dinner party, a picnic, a drink at the local or even a country walk, if the weather is right and they all enjoy that sort of exercise, would give them all a chance to talk and get to know one another well.

A visit to a theatre or any entertainment that prevents the best man and the chief bridesmaid from talking together, is not recommended.

They each have equivalent responsibilities; the chief bridesmaid to the bride – and the best man and his ushers to the bridegroom. And each will require to know the arrangements of the other if both parties to the wedding are to dovetail harmoniously.

It is not so easily solved when the home of the bride is some considerable way from that of the bridegroom and his best man. As it is likely that the bride has chosen her chief bridesmaid from the girls in that locality – and, of course, the wedding will in all probability take place in the bride's home town – it will be more difficult for the best man and the chief bridesmaid to meet. However, if it is possible the bridegroom should arrange for his best man to accompany him on one of his trips to the home of his fiancée with the object of getting the chief bridesmaid together with the best man.

The best man has no official status in the advance arrangements being made for the engagement party, the stag party, the wedding or the reception – though, of course, he has important duties to perform at both the service and the reception afterwards.

The engagement party is entirely the affair of the bride and her future husband; the stag party is arranged by the bridegroom, though he may require the assistance of his best man (though sometimes the best man may arrange it); the wedding is arranged by the bridegroom and his future wife in consultation with the incumbent of the church concerned – and the reception to follow is booked – and eventually paid for – by the bride's parents.

Before the wedding the best man is concerned chiefly in seeing to it that the bridegroom is preparing himself for his wedding, so he is busy:

(a) Appointing the ushers in consultation with the bridegroom.

(b) Making sure of the degree of formality expected at the wedding and seeing to it that the bridegroom obtains the right clothing for the occasion. At the same time he will instruct the ushers accordingly and order his own wedding garments, and arrange to collect them the day before the wedding.

(c) Helping the bridegroom with the arrangements for the stag party – if he is asked; and clearing up afterwards.

(d) Ordering a wedding car for himself and the bridegroom if one is required, and arranging another car for the newly-weds for their departure after the reception.

(e) Checking that the buttonholes for the bride-groom, best man and ushers have been included in the bride's order to the florist.

On the morning of the wedding the best man must:

(a) If they are not to be delivered, pick up the buttonholes for himself and the bridegroom.

(b) Dress in his full wedding regalia first, leaving himself free to attend the bridegroom from then on.

(c) Conduct the possibly nervous bridegroom to the church.

(d) Be the custodian of the wedding ring until the moment it is required to seal the marriage.

(e) Take charge of the honeymoon documents and the bridegroom's luggage.

At the church he will:

(a) Take the bridegroom to his ordained place at the foot of the chancel steps.

(b) Hand over the wedding ring (or rings) at the appropriate moment during the service.

Hand over the wedding ring at the appropriate moment.

(c) Go to the vestry after the service, to sign the marriage register as a witness.

(d) Marshal the wedding party for the photographer at the church door.

(e) Usher the newly-weds into their car.

(f) Pay the marriage fees, if this has not been done.

After the service the best man must hurry to the venue of the reception and:

(a) Help to marshal the guests towards the receiving line.

(b) Act as toastmaster, unless a professional toastmaster is employed.

(c) Reply to the toast of 'the bridesmaids'.

(d) Read out the telemessages of congratulations that have been received by the bridal couple.

(e) Return to the bridegroom the travel documents in connection with the honeymoon.

(f) See the couple – and their luggage – to their car or taxi. And their departure.

(g) Speed the parting guests and, if required, escort the bridesmaids to their homes.

(h) Collect the bridegroom's discarded wedding clothes and, if necessary, return them as soon as possible to the hire firm.

(i) Help to collect and transport the wedding presents to the home of the bride's parents, if needed.

5

The Wedding Regalia

Various degrees of formality are reflected in the dress of the participants in a wedding ceremony. These variations are usually dictated by the previous marital status of the bride and bridegroom; sometimes age takes the overriding urge for 'show' out of the procedure; often because few guests can be expected, perhaps because of the distant venue of the service from the homes of the parties concerned; sometimes because of the lack of time between the decision to marry and the ceremony itself and there are occasions when the scale of the wedding is controlled by financial resources.

The formal outfit for the bridegroom, the best man and the ushers is 'morning coat'. This is not commonly used these days. It comprises:

(a) Black morning coat.
(b) Grey striped trousers – without turn-ups.
(c) Grey waistcoat – usually double-breasted with lapels.
(d) Grey tie – the cravat is rarely worn today.
(e) White shirt – with a turn-down collar.
(f) Black socks and shoes.
(g) A white handkerchief in the breast pocket.

There are variations in fashion all over the world, and indeed from one part of Britain to another. A style that has become more fashionable is a grey morning suit (with tails). A cravat is sometimes worn with this, and grey socks and black shoes are worn. It is up to the bridegroom to conform to the style of the moment, and of the locality.

It is not, however, necessary for formal dress to be worn. A suit is just as acceptable nowadays.

Unless the wedding is almost a 'State occasion', the formality of dress does not apply to everyone present. Those who are expected to conform with the bridegroom (who sets the fashion) are:

(a) The best man who must support the bridegroom.

(b) The bride's father who will be in the forefront at his daughter's side.

(c) The ushers.

(d) The groom's father.

If the wedding is of the 'fashionable' degree, these too should be added to the list of those expected to dress in the same fashion as the bridegroom – though they need not do so if the wedding is of lesser interest to the general public:

(a) The bridegroom's brothers.

(b) The bride's brothers.

(c) Other close family relatives.

(d) Friends who happen to be well-known figures in the neighbourhood.

Other male guests may please themselves as to what they wear, but lounge suits are preferable.

Grey wedding 'toppers', though still worn, have

become a thing of the past – though no other form of headgear may be worn with a morning coat at a wedding.

It is almost impossible to wear them in the modern, low-roofed car or taxi on the way to and from the church and the reception rooms; nor can they, of course, be worn indoors.

In fact the 'topper' is usually more of a nuisance than a decoration – and even a worry. Imagine having, after the service in the church, to find your top-hat from amongst a stack of others, all exactly similar and most of them bearing, as the only means of identification, the same maker's label!

As the only chance of wearing a hat comes during the very few moments spent in getting into and out of cars, and the more lengthy period spent on photographs at the church door, it is purposeless being burdened with a hat of any kind – unless you are subject to colds, of course.

The more informal weddings are not necessarily the less solemn nor, to the happy couple, less important than those staged in the height of fashion.

Even though the bride may wear her wedding gown with its train and veil, there is no reason why the interested parties should not agree on a more relaxed style for the men.

In such cases the bridegroom, his best man and indeed all male members of the wedding party, should be dressed in lounge suits. In full, the dress normally comprises:

(a) A lounge suit of the current style (usually light in colour).

(b) The waistcoat should be of the same material though this item is often omitted, especially in the spring and summer.

Different forms of dress:

Left: Formal – suitable for a 'posh' wedding.
Middle: Smart suit – suitable for most normal weddings.
Right: Donkey-jacket – not suitable for a wedding at all.

(c) The trousers should be of the same material – so that the suit in full is entirely suitable for normal wear instead of having to be put to one side after the wedding.

(d) Shirt with a turn-down collar.

(e) Socks and shoes, in accordance with the rest of the attire.

(f) A handkerchief showing from the breast pocket, colour to blend with the suit.

(g) A tie, usually silk, to go with the suit.

Yet again it is wise to consult a tailor as to the very latest fashion. Such trivial items as to whether the jacket should have two or three buttons, the lapels wide or narrow and the trouser bottoms turned up or down vary almost monthly – and might even tend to cause embarrassment if one of the party should find himself dressed differently from the others.

The only other item of wear that should not be omitted for a wedding is the buttonhole. It is often a white carnation, but nowadays it is quite in order for men to wear buttonholes that enhance their suits – it might be a red rose, or a red, yellow or pink carnation. It has been known for a florist to provide a black buttonhole to go with an all white suit! Very often the bridegroom, best man and the two fathers will have one colour buttonhole and the ushers and any other male members of the wedding party another colour so that they can be easily identified especially if they are all wearing grey 'penguin' suits.

Most male guests should wear buttonholes, and they can be expected to provide their own.

One other worrisome feature of the dress regulations concerning the male members of the wedding party can be the expense involved. It certainly seems a waste of money to buy a morning suit that will probably be worn only a very few times in a lifetime – possibly on a single occasion.

However, it is a simple matter today to hire the suit for the day for a few pounds – and it is now almost the universal practice to do so, even by the bridegroom and his best man.

Moss Bros. of Covent Garden, London, WC2 are well known for their hire service. They have branches or agents throughout Britain and they also operate a postal service from London.

The demand for this service is widespread and it is important to make arrangements for the hire of such garments well in advance of the date they are actually required – if you are to obtain a first-class fit. And it is equally important to return the outfit immediately the hire period is up as it will need 'refreshing' before being passed on to the next anxiously waiting customer. Most hire firms work on a 'Friday to Monday' basis.

6

The Stag Party

Before the day of the wedding the best man may find himself attending a number of usually intimate parties concerned with the event.

Some brides and their grooms fight shy of too much ostentation in this direction, preferring to save their energies – and perhaps their finances – for the 'big' day. Others, perhaps more gregarious, run the gamut of the possible private parties.

There will probably be the engagement party, a small get-together to introduce the best man and the chief bridesmaid to one another, the family party where both sets of parents are brought together and which the best man and the chief bridesmaid may well be expected to attend. There may even be a 'we were all unmarried friends' affair – but *last* of them all as far as the bridegroom and his best man are concerned, is the stag party.

It is at this affair the bridegroom entertains for the last time his bachelor friends – a serio-comic affair, full of mock-nostalgia and high-spirited finality.

The origin of the custom of holding such a party appears to be lost somewhere deep amongst the mysterious wedding superstitions of old. The idea seems to have arisen as nothing more serious than the wish of a gathering of friends to say a mocking farewell to him amongst them who was about to sacrifice his freedom for the doubtful state of married bliss. A last fling before a bridegroom assumed the mantle of responsibility and comes under the sobering influence of a feminine partner – putting an end to the 'wild oats' period of his life.

At one time the stag party was invariably scheduled for the eve of the wedding – sometimes with disastrous results.

By the very nature of the party and the fact that it is a 'men only' affair, the gathering will almost certainly become a high-spirited affair – with the distinct

The aftermath.

possibility of a few 'hangovers' on the following morning.

As this is the morning of the wedding it can be a sad and anxious morning for a somewhat distrait bridegroom, an uneasy – and queasy – period for the best man and many of the guests who had attended the previous night's party – and most distressing to the bride.

In fact, particularly in the days of the Prince Regent – and often enough since – it was not unknown for a man to have to be conducted to the altar by a best man almost as unfit to stand up as the bridegroom himself; neither of them in a fit condition to follow the details of the service. And almost as often, in great-great-grandfather's time, the 'hairs-of-a-biting-dog' taken before the wedding and at the reception afterwards, forced upon a bridegroom by misguided friends, has resulted in as many brides finding themselves tearfully alone on their wedding night, while their sadly inebriated husbands have slept stertorously and soundly through the night.

Fortunately, and possibly at the instigation of many an unhappy bride, it has now become the custom to hold the stag party some days in advance of the wedding – leaving plenty of time for recuperation and return to the eager anticipation of the great day.

It is the bridegroom's prerogative to invite only his own, unmarried male friends to the stag party. As his best friend, of course, the best man will be the first to be asked, but his official duties will be minimal. In fact, apart from general 'assistance' the best man's only responsibilities are to sit at the foot of the table from where he will have to make a speech, and finally to help the bridegroom see his guests off – not forgetting the possible need to escort the bridegroom himself, home.

The guests generally consist of the bridegroom's close friends – among whom he can be expected to invite his unmarried brothers – and, if he is wise, his bride's unmarried brothers. The actual numbers must depend on the number of friends claimed by the groom – and his financial resources.

Although custom decrees that the guests are all bachelors – and at one time this restriction was mandatory – it is often ignored nowadays to make way for very close friends and relatives who happen to be married. They will all be young, of course – and no females will be admitted under any circumstances.

In general practice the guests, though of the same generation as the bridegroom, should not be under the age of 17; 18 is a more realistic age, where possible, in view of the prohibitions laid down by the Liquor Licensing Laws.

The party is an informal affair as often as not, though in some circles it is still expected that the guests will wear dinner jackets. The party may be a simple get-together in a private room in a 'pub'; it may be held in a private reception room at some hotel – or it may even be staged in the home of the bridegroom's parents (in which event the parents will expect to have to go 'elsewhere' for the evening).

It may include a full-scale dinner, often it is a cocktail party with snacks – and on occasion it is no more than 'a few drinks amongst friends'.

The main speech of the evening is expected to be made by the best man, either at the coffee stage of the dinner or at the 'between' stage when sufficient liquor has been consumed – but not too much.

The speech should be of the nature of an entertainment; humorous, full of happy stories, slanted to poke as much fun as possible at the bridegroom.

This is one of the occasions where the best man should show his capacity for the duties he has undertaken and show his leadership in the series of events that lead up to, and follow, the wedding.

Unless he is extremely quick-witted with an unusually fast-moving mind, the best man should prepare in advance the text of his speech and if necessary rehearse it to the point where it sounds free and 'off the cuff' – and unrehearsed.

The contents must be amusing, anecdotal and entirely concerned with the bridegroom and his friends. It must be made at sufficient length, but not to the extent of beginning to bore the listeners.

Points that may be used in such a speech include:

(a) Some amusing incidents of the bridegroom's childhood.

(b) The unfortunate girls that are now to be abandoned by the bridegroom – and the difficulties in getting rid of them.

(c) The idea that two can live as cheaply as one being a fallacy.

(d) Some of the means whereby he can escape his fate; the river, an overdose – or perhaps a slow boat to the Orient.

The bridegroom's reply should be the only other speech of the evening – and if there is any entertainment to follow, it should be brought on at this stage.

An entertainment is not really necessary at such a party though it is occasionally added, particularly if there are any theatrical people present. Generally, by the time the speeches have been made – and sufficient liquor consumed – the entertainment becomes self-made.

The host should be the last to leave the party – usually in company with his best man. And the best man should be in a fit state to warn their friends about their condition to drive – and finally, if necessary, take the bridegroom home in a taxi.

7

The Wedding Eve

The day preceding the wedding is a busy one for all concerned – not least, for the best man. He is likely to be required to help the bridegroom in all sorts of unexpected directions – as often as not to soothe away some unnecessary worry – and to assist the bride in matters between herself and her future husband. 'Has he remembered to . . .', 'You haven't let him forget . . .?' and 'Do see to it that he . . .' are all growing symptoms of wedding day nerves.

Before he becomes too involved in personal problems posed by any and everybody associated with the wedding, it is well for the best man to check on the preparations for which he will be held responsible. He should leave nothing to chance and amongst the more important queries he should make are:

(a) Has the florist got the order for the buttonholes required by the bridegroom and himself? And as it is probable that the ushers and some of the male guests have asked for their buttonholes to be added to the order, check on them too.

(b) Collect the hired suits for both the bridegroom and himself.

(c) Make sure that all items of apparel, other than

any hired suits, are already in his own wardrobe and that of the bridegroom, as well as shirts, socks, ties, and clean handkerchiefs.

(d) That there has been no slip-up in the order for taxis – and their exact timetable. They may be wanted to carry the best man and the groom to the church, to convey the newly-weds from the church to the reception, with a second for the use of the best man, enabling him to escort a bevy of bridesmaids to the same place and on occasion a third and fourth car will be needed to take both sets of parents, and any elderly relatives from the church to the reception. And if the bridal couple are to leave from the reception rooms for their honeymoon by taxi – an order must be placed for that too.

(e) That the bridegroom is in possession of the wedding ring. No doubt his bride has seen to its purchase – but has he got it in his keeping?

(f) Has the bridegroom collected together the honeymoon documents? Check them to make sure that none have been forgotten. The best man will undoubtedly be blamed if the newly-weds arrive at Las Palmas – or wherever their destination is – to find that they have either left behind their travellers' cheques or omitted to obtain any in the first place.

Depending on the honeymoon resort and the mode of travel, documents may well include credit card or travellers' cheques, passports; rail, ferry and/or air tickets; hotel reservation confirmations and excursion tickets. As this list is by no means exhaustive it would be well if the bridegroom got together with the best man and listed them well in advance – so that this last-minute check can be made with certainty.

(g) That the bridegroom has completed the main part of his packing for the honeymoon journey – leaving only, for the following morning, such things as last-minute toilet items and the clothing he intends to change into from his wedding outfit.

The best man should make an opportunity during the day to call on the bride's mother to collect the Order of Service sheets required for distribution in the church and should allow time for being roped in by the bride's family for various chores. By this time, the best man should have been in touch with each usher and told them roughly what their duties will be, and the time they should be at the church. He should arrange to meet the chief usher to hand over the Order of Service Sheets with any other last-minute details, sometime during the day. The chief usher will receive instructions whether to offer an Order of Service Sheet to each guest as they enter the church and are escorted to their seats, or whether they should be placed on each seat in the church before the guests arrive.

Guidance may have to be given as to the proper way to greet the guests and the correct places among the pews in which each should be seated.

The customary seating arrangements for the wedding guests are detailed on page 16.

The best man may now feel himself free to deal with the less official burdens that will undoubtedly be thrust in his direction; in the first instance by the bridegroom who will certainly claim a proprietary right to his services, and as convenient afterwards, by everyone else who may have some part to play in the following day's events.

The bride's calls for the best man's assistance may be frequent, particularly if she has no brothers to help her – and he may be sure that the main calls will concern 'porterage'.

'Can you collect the cake from the bakers and deliver it to the caterer at the reception rooms, please?' she will ask – if the confectioner does not make his own deliveries. 'There is still all this going-away luggage to be taken down to the changing room at the hotel where we are having the reception. Perhaps you could take it there at the same time?' 'And what about the wedding presents? They all have to be taken down to the reception rooms where we've arranged for them to be displayed?'

This latter request is likely to be quite a time-taker. No doubt the bride and her mother will direct the build-up of the display, but of course a man will be needed to do the chores.

The usual method of arranging this exhibition of wedding presents is to set up tables in a room set aside

Exhibition of wedding gifts.

for the purpose; the number of tables depending, of course, on the number and size of the gifts.

The tables should be covered with white tablecloths and perhaps tiered with the aid of large boxes decorated with coloured crêpe paper – or, of course, the white tablecloths.

The presents usually need to be removed from their packages – though the cartons should be retained so that the items can be transported to the bride's home eventually, without damage.

Each gift should be identified by a white card, as often as not sent with it, set up beside the piece on the show tables. They should be inscribed with the donor's name and address, and perhaps the relationship of the giver to the bride or the bridegroom.

It is quite possible that a number of wedding presents take the form of a cheque. In such cases, as with gifts of insurance policies, share certificates, or possibly the deeds of a house, for safety's sake the cheques should be banked as soon as possible, and certificates, etc., put in a safe place. For display purposes, the donors' names can be listed on a piece of card, but the amount should never be shown, i.e.:

Cheques have been received from:
 Mr. & Mrs John Green and Alexandra
 Mr. & Mrs. Robert Walker
etc.

Someone should be held responsible for locking the door of the room where the presents are being displayed and safeguarding the key until the following day.

Alternatively in this era of the increasing need for security precautions it may be better not to have the wedding gifts on display in a hotel, or in a hall during

the reception. Either the bride's mother, or the bride –
if she is fortunate enough to move straight into a home
of her own – might have the gifts on display in their
home and can send out cards (available from
stationers) as follows:

> 10 Bow Road,
> HORLEY,
> Surrey, RH1 7QL

Dear ......
   We would like to express our sincere thanks for your
kind wishes and most acceptable gift.
   Would you please come to our Show of Presents on
Wednesday, 17th September at 7.30 p.m.

> Jane and Mark

8

The Wedding Morning

Whatever the scheduled time of the wedding, the best man must be up and about at an early hour. He will probably dress in utility clothes to save time while he gathers together the numerous items required by the bridegroom and himself – and not forgetting any commissions he has promised to undertake for the bride.

Probably the first call will be a hurried visit to the bridegroom's home to check that all is well, followed by a rush around to the bride's home to carry out any errands for her, and to collect the buttonholes.

Back to his own home to dress in his own wedding regalia and to ensure, in good time, that he has all the items required by a best man for the performance of his task.

The main requirement at this stage is to ensure that he has in his pocket sufficient funds to meet the various fees connected with the wedding if they have not already been paid. It is unlikely that this will be refunded by the bridegroom until his return from his honeymoon!

The most frustrating part of a best man's duties at this stage, particularly if the bridegroom is inclined to be nervous and over-anxious, is to attend on him during the last stages of his preparation for the ceremony.

The best man should have plenty of time in hand when he arrives at the home of the bridegroom, already fully dressed and ready for the journey to the church.

The first thing is to get the bridegroom into his wedding outfit – leaving time to deal with the emergencies, caused by forgetfulness, that will almost surely arise. The missing button, a broken shoe-lace, a badly crumpled tie – any one of a hundred trivial items that can go adrift and mar the 'big' day.

Ask the bridegroom's mother to pin the buttonholes into place.

If the bridegroom's mother is going to be asked to pin the buttonholes into place – as only a woman can –

the best man should remember that she and her family are due at the church early and must leave home some time in advance.

As soon as he is satisfied that the bridegroom is properly dressed, the best man should check and take charge of the following items:

(a) The wedding ring or rings – which are best placed in a waistcoat pocket, deliberately selected so that the best man will not forget where he put them and have to start an undignified search of his pockets at the very moment he is due to place them on the Prayer Book, in the hands of the minister.

(b) The various documents required for the honeymoon as gathered together on the previous day.

(c) After ensuring that the bridegroom has completed his packing for the journey with his bride, the best man should take temporary charge of the suitcases – and the keys.

(d) Make certain that the bridegroom packs all the clothing he will need in which to change after the reception and in which he will travel. These must, of course, be packed separately – and again, placed in the care of the best man.

If the best man still finds himself with time in hand and is not likely to be delayed by traffic conditions, he should take the opportunity of running the suitcases to the scene of the reception and depositing them there ready for the departure of the newly-weds.

Perhaps a happier alternative to this is for the best man to persuade one of the ushers to collect the suitcases at the bridegroom's home and convey them to the reception rooms – so long as he leaves himself plenty of time to arrive at the church before the first of the guests.

A less reliable, though often practised method, is for the bridegroom and his best man to make a diversion on their way to the church, to deliver the cases. This can lead to anxiety about time-keeping that may well depress the pair.

As soon as all these preparations are complete, the time arrives for the bridegroom and his best man to pace nervously about the room, waiting for the arrival of the taxi. The fact that it may not be due for another ten minutes will do little to ease the niggle of worry in their minds.

'I'll bet it's going to be late,' prophesies the bridegroom.

'It's the traffic that worries me,' sighs the best man. 'There's a football match on in town so there's sure to be a hold up.'

'You're sure you didn't forget to order it?'

'Of course I didn't – but that doesn't say you can rely on it getting back from some previous journey on time.'

'There could have been an accident.'

But despite all the doubts, it is more than probable that the driver will knock on your door within one minute of the time arranged. And as he is both an expert on the route and in forecasting the traffic flow, he will deposit the bridegroom and the best man at the door of the church right on time.

'On time' should mean fifteen to twenty minutes before the bride is due to arrive on the arm of her father – or if she has no father, of whoever is to give her away.

If the best man and groom are driving to the church together, the best man should, at the very least, check that he has enough petrol to get to the church on time.

9

The Ceremony

The Church of England

Having arrived at the church on time, the bridegroom and his best man should find themselves some out-of-the-way spot where they can wait in peace until it is time for them to take their places. The clergyman often takes this opportunity to invite the bridegroom to check the details for the register, and this is a convenient time to settle any unpaid fees.

If the groom and best man are wearing hats and gloves, they should be placed conveniently for the best man to carry both his and the bridegroom's to the vestry after the service.

As soon as he has satisfied himself that the bridegroom is likely to remain undisturbed, the best man should give himself a few minutes to ensure that the ushers are receiving the wedding guests at the church door, conducting them to their pews and handing out the Order of Service sheets. He should make sure, and help if necessary, to break up any tendency on the part of the guests to stop and chat in the church porch, so holding up the seating of the congregation and blocking the entrance. This is especially important if the wedding is a large one.

It is always a temptation for guests and relatives, who may not have met for a long time, to greet one another fulsomely and at length.

'It must be all of twenty years,' says one.

'And how is your daughter? Moira, isn't it?'

'Maud. She's fine, but didn't you hear? She's married. Has a fine baby boy of her own now.'

'Well I never. And your own son, didn't he become an architect?'

'An archaeologist, as a matter of fact. His will be the next wedding, I expect. Such a nice girl. You probably remember her mother Jean Blake. Thompson, she was.'

And so on, and so on. And can you blame them?
A little tact will go a long way to persuade people to withhold their family reminiscences until the reception that is due to take place after the service.

The chief bridesmaid is due to arrive five minutes ahead of the bride – accompanied by the rest of the bridesmaids and, if there are any, the pages. The best man should not stay to talk to her but accept this as his signal to return to the bridegroom down a side aisle if available and to conduct him quietly and slowly to be seated in the front right-hand side pew until the wedding procession arrives at the church door.
For the next two or three minutes the bridegroom will cast anxious glances over his shoulder towards the church door in search of his bride. 'Is she going to turn up?' no doubt will pass through his mind – while the best man nervously fingers the wedding rings to make

Arrival of bridesmaids and page.

sure – for the fiftieth time, no doubt – that they have not vanished.

This is the one time in her life that the bride is expected to arrive exactly on time. The bride who arrives early can cause great panic. If necessary, the driver must be instructed to make some detour so as to arrive on time. If she is late, apart from the slight to her waiting groom, it might well be interpreted as discourtesy by the clergyman, the officials and the guests.

Besides, and even more important, it is possible that another wedding is due to follow immediately afterwards – and a late start must mean a hurried, even garbled service, or complete disorganisation for the other unhappy couple.

Suddenly, as the organist will have been warned of the arrival of the bride, the church will be filled with the first notes of one of the wedding marches and as the congregation stands the bridegroom and best man should move towards the chancel steps where they will stand facing the altar. The bridegroom should leave room on his left for the bride who will arrive on her father's right arm. The best man should stand on the bridegroom's right.

The bridegroom and best man should turn to welcome the bride as she approaches in procession down the aisle when the bridesmaids follow the bride two by two, led by the chief bridesmaid. If there are any pages they are likely to be tiny tots who may either march ahead of the bridesmaids – after the chief bridesmaid – or, if their attention is likely to wander, paired off with the bridesmaids.

The bride and father process down the aisle.

As the bride reaches her groom's side, he and the best man should turn to face the clergyman who will, more usually, move to his place as the procession approaches down the aisle.

As the bridal party come to a standstill, the organ will fade out leaving silence for the clergyman. The chief bridesmaid should step forward as the bride's father frees his daughter's arm, take the bride's bouquet, lift the veil back from her face and adjust her train if necessary. She then returns to her place behind the bride.

At this point there is commonly a hymn which allows everybody a chance to settle any last minute nerves.

ASB (Alternative Service Book) 1980 provides for a prayer and bible reading at this point if desired.

The clergyman then begins the ordained service by:

1. Stating the reason for the gathering in the church.
2. The reason for matrimony.
3. Demanding to know if there are any impediments to the marriage; first from the congregation and then from the bridal couple. (Any objector may be required to furnish a bond as an earnest of good faith.)

If no valid objections are voiced the clergyman will then ask the bridegroom:

'Wilt thou have this Woman to thy wedded wife, to live together according to God's law in the holy estate of Matrimony? Wilt thou love her, comfort her, honour and keep her in sickness and in health; and, forsaking all other, keep thee only unto her, so long as ye both shall live?'

The bridegroom answers: 'I will.'

ALTAR

CHOIR STALLS

CHOIR STALLS

MINISTER

GROOM

BEST MAN

BRIDE'S FATHER   BRIDE

PEWS

PEWS

BRIDE'S

BRIDEGROOM'S

RELATIONS

RELATIONS

AND FRIENDS

AND FRIENDS

BRIDESMAIDS

Position as the bride's procession reaches the front of the aisles.

ALTAR

CHOIR STALLS

CHOIR STALLS

MINISTER

BRIDE GROOM

BRIDE'S FATHER

BEST MAN

CHIEF BRIDESMAID

PEWS

PEWS

BRIDE'S

BRIDEGROOM'S

BRIDESMAIDS

RELATIONS

RELATIONS

AND FRIENDS

AND FRIENDS

Positions during the ceremony.

The clergyman then asks the bride:

'Wilt though have this Man to thy wedded husband, to live together according to God's law in the holy estate of Matrimony? Wilt thou love him, comfort him, honour and keep him in sickness and health; and forsaking all other, keep thee only to him, so long as ye both shall live?'

The bride answers: 'I will.'

The clergyman will then ask:

'Who giveth this Woman to be married to this Man?'

The bride's father (or whoever is giving her away) should not, but very often does, answer: 'I do.'

The bride's father passes his daughter's right hand to the clergyman, palm downwards. The clergyman passes it into the right hand of the bridegroom.

The bride's father takes no further part in the service and he may now, if he so wishes, drop back and take his place in the front pew beside his wife – though more commonly, it is the practice to remain at his daughter's side until after the clergyman has pronounced the couple man and wife and given them a blessing. The important thing is that if he moves it should be as unobtrusively as possible.

The bridegroom will now say after the clergyman, repeating phrase by phrase:

'I ...... take thee, ... to my wedded wife, to have and to hold from this day forward, for better for worse, for richer for poorer, in sickness and in health, to love and to cherish, till death us do part; according to God's holy law, and thereto I give thee my troth.'

The pair will free their hands and then the bride will take the right hand of the bridegroom in her own right hand and say after the clergyman, repeating phrase by phrase:

'I ...... take thee, ... to my wedded husband, to have and to hold from this day forward, for better for worse, for richer for poorer, in sickness and in health, to love and to cherish, till death us do part, according to God's holy law, and thereto I give thee my troth.'

As they free their hands, the best man takes the wedding ring or rings from his pocket and places them on the open page of the Prayer Book proffered by the

The Best Man places the ring on the prayer book.

clergyman. After a prayer for the blessing of the ring the clergyman will offer the ring to the bridegroom who will take it and place it on the third finger of the bride's left hand.

Neither the engagement nor any other ring should be worn on that finger during the service – and, in fact, it is usual to wear no ring on that hand until the wedding ring has been placed there.

While the bridegroom holds the ring in place on the bride's finger, he will repeat after the clergyman:

'With this Ring I thee wed, with my body I thee honour, and all my worldly goods with thee I share: In the Name of the Father, and of the Son, and of the Holy Ghost. Amen.'

It is sometimes the case these days that the bride wishes to give a ring to the bridegroom. When this is so, the best man gives both rings to the clergyman and they are both blessed. The bride puts the ring on the bridegroom's finger after she herself has received the ring he is giving her, but without any words being spoken, or both may repeat the words together.

The 1928 Prayer Book is now replaced by Alternative Services, Series 1. The Alternative Service Book 1980 has promises in more modern language either with or without the word 'obey', and the couple are given the choice of which wording they prefer to use.

The wedding is now complete but it is usually followed by the nuptial blessing, prayers and psalm.

The clergyman or verger then leads the way to the vestry or side chapel followed by the newly-married couple, the best man brings his own hat and gloves as well as those of the bridegroom if these are being worn, and the chief bridesmaid brings the bride's bouquet. The parents of both the bride and groom usually follow into the vestry to watch the signing of the register.

The bride signs the register.

In the vestry or side chapel the bride will sign the register using her maiden name for the last time – though legally she may choose whether or not to take her husband's name. Her husband adds his signature followed by the clergyman and the two witnesses selected for the purpose. The selection of the two witnesses should have been made some time in advance and usually comprises the best man and the chief bridesmaid provided that they are not under the age of 18 years.

As the guests will be waiting in the body of the church to see the bridal couple leave, only the briefest congratulations are in order in the vestry.

Again the organist will receive some secret signal, denoting that the bridal party are ready for the recessional and will break into the appropriate march.

ALTAR

CHOIR STALLS

CHOIR STALLS

BRIDE'S FATHER

GROOM'S MOTHER

GROOM'S FATHER

BRIDE'S MOTHER

PEWS

PEWS

BRIDE'S

BRIDEGROOM'S

BRIDESMAIDS

RELATIONS

RELATIONS

AND FRIENDS

AND FRIENDS

GROOM

BRIDE

The recession after the service.

The bridegroom, with the bride on his left arm, will lead the way from the vestry or chapel and followed by those present with them, in the same order as they entered. There is one exception to this where the layout permits – the best man will leave as early as he can and make his way to the church door by the quickest route, in time to meet the couple as they reach the porch. Otherwise he walks with the chief bridesmaid.

There is likely to be some delay at this point. If the weather is fine no doubt arrangements will have been made by the bride and her mother for the attendance of a photographer. He will wish to pose the happy couple for his camera and probably expect to be able to add photographs of the bridesmaids and the best man in attendance upon them, and the full bridal party – mothers, fathers and grandparents too.

Then will come the spate of photographs demanded by the amateur photographers. According to their relationship to the bridal pair or to whom they are closely associated, they will demand single snaps; bride and bridesmaids only; the bridegroom with his best man and ushers; the couple alone, etc., etc., so long as there are spare films in the cameras.

As the unofficial master of ceremonies at this stage, the best man needs to keep a close watch on the time. The whole party will be due at the reception at some scheduled time and if the guests are late in arrival, they may find themselves reduced to having a cold meal and being rushed so that the newly-weds can catch a plane.

As soon as he can persuade the party and their guests to start moving, the best man must see the bridal couple to their car and check that the bride has received the marriage certificate from the clergyman. The bride and groom are expected to leave the precincts of the church first – followed by other cars carrying their parents, bridesmaids, family and then the guests.

Photography.

As the ushers are closing the car doors on the less important guests, the best man should collect the marriage certificate if the bride has not already done so. If it is not convenient for her to take it before she leaves for her honeymoon, the best man should hand it over to the bride's mother.

The best man should take the opportunity, before he leaves the church, to ensure that the bridegroom's expenses have been settled, i.e. the marriage fees; the clergyman's fee, the organist's fee and not forgetting the verger. It is usually convenient for the best man to settle these accounts through the verger – the fee for the clergyman being handed over in a sealed envelope at the same time.

All fees are nowadays usually settled well before the day, but, if not, the best man does this duty. If there is no opportunity for him to have a word with the clergyman afterwards, there is no objection to the fees being placed in a sealed envelope and given to the verger to be delivered in due course. Fees are generally paid in one lump.

Confetti should not be strewn in the churchyard, simply because of good manners – never mind the laws regarding litter! It should be reserved for after the reception as the couple leave.

Before we leave the church for the reception, the following points may be of interest:

(a) During the procession down the nave the bride's veil should shield her face – and her attention and that of her attendants should be directed towards the chancel steps and the waiting bridegroom with his best man.

During the recessional from the vestry, along the nave and to the church door, the bride's veil will be clear of her face – and it is permissible for her and her bridegroom to smile and nod to their friends, but there must be no pause or conversation until they are beyond the church door.

(b) It is widely believed that women must have their heads covered in a church, but in fact it is a custom and not an obligation. This freedom now applies to the Church of England, the Roman Catholic Church and some of the free churches but not in the case of a Jewish Synagogue.

(c) It is generally possible where there are bells to have them pealed for twenty minutes immediately prior to the service and for up to half and hour afterwards, but of course a fee will be due to the bellringers. The organist and the verger should be consulted on the point.

As soon as the best man has settled the financial matters in connection with the marriage, he must hurry along to the reception where he will be needed. It is well for him either to have a taxi standing by at his sole disposal or to have a car of his own immediately available.

Where the bride happens to be a *widow*, the wedding itself takes precisely the same form as that for a 'first' marriage, though it is traditional to expect less formality and the omission of much of the pageantry.

It is usual, though by no means obligatory, for the bride to forego the bridal gown, and the veil. Nor is she attended by a coterie of bridesmaids; even the chief bridesmaid is replaced by a 'dame (or matron) of honour'. The order of selection is a (perhaps married) sister of the bride as the first choice, failing which a sister of the bridegroom is chosen or, as a last resort, a close friend.

In deference to the bride's lack of formal attire, the bridegroom and his best man will wear 'lounge' suits as will the ushers, if any are appointed.

The bridal bouquet and the buttonholes for the men are still customary.

The procession is considered to be too formal for such a wedding and it is usual for the matron-of-honour to join the bridegroom and the best man at the foot of the chancel steps, there to await the arrival of the bride, on her father's arm or that of another male relative, at their ordained place in front of the officiating clergyman. Nor is it necessary for the bride to walk down the aisle under the gaze of the guests; it is quite usual for her to arrive early with her father or other male relative and to sit in a front-row pew until the time comes for her to step forward to the side of her bridegroom.

The number of guests invited to the wedding and the reception afterwards is a matter of arrangement between the bride and her groom, though the time that has elapsed since the death of the bride's previous husband must be taken into consideration when the decision is made. If:

(a) The bride has been a widow for less than a year, the custom is to invite the parents of both parties to the wedding, a best man and a matron-of-honour. Invitations to friends should be restricted to only those who are close – the actual number being fewer and fewer, the shorter the period of widowhood. If, for some reason, the wedding takes place within a matter of weeks of the death of her previous husband, the invitations should be strictly limited to whoever is to give the bride away, a matron-of-honour, the best man and at the most, four to six friends or relatives.

(b) The generally accepted mourning period for a wife is considered to be a full year – and if this period has elapsed before her 'second' wedding is due to take place, no limitations are placed on the number of guests who may be invited both to the service and the reception afterwards – though the pageantry of the actual ceremony is still restricted to a less formal affair than for a 'first' wedding.

Whatever the bride decides to wear for her wedding, 'white' is considered to be suitable only for a 'first' marriage – and is definitely out of place for a widow.

A *widower* is subject to far fewer restrictions when he marries for the second time, than is a widow. Though it is customary to restrict the pageantry usually associated with a first wedding, the style and scale of the event may be left to the bride and her parents. After all, it may be her first wedding; if so she has the right to wear a bridal gown and a veil and be followed to the altar by a retinue of bridesmaids – if she should so wish. In fact she may demand the full panoply of the occasion and expect to get it – so long as the bridegroom's first wife has been dead for more than a year.

If this period of mourning has been shorter than the customary period, the bride should consider limiting her 'rights' in the decision as to the manner of her wedding. Much more acceptable to the public, would be her insistence that a full year should pass before her bridegroom made his second venture into matrimony.

The Church of England does not permit the remarriage of *divorced persons* and no clergyman of that faith may be .compelled to permit anyone else to use his church in which to perform such a ceremony. This restriction is equally applicable where the marriage is concerned with either two divorced persons, or the marriage of a divorced man or woman to a single person. Clergymen can be found who are prepared to ignore ecclesiastical authority and perform such a ceremony. Others will arrange a church service of blessing following a civil ceremony.

The Civil Law in Britain, however, does recognise the remarriage of divorced persons – in fact, if there are no other legal objections and the statutory requirements are carried out, a Superintendent Registrar may not refuse to conduct such a ceremony, though it will probably have to be conducted in a Register Office.

A Marriage in a Register Office, before a Superintendent Registrar is necessarily a simple affair and takes but a few minutes to complete – though it is as legally binding as that performed before a minister of religion.

The wedding consists of little other than the exchange of vows between the bride and bridegroom and as no religious service is involved, this leaves nothing more to be done than the signing of the register by the newly-married couple and their witnesses – and the collection of the marriage certificate.

Though the wedding reception to follow is normally an intimate affair, it might be that the wedding is not concerned with the more usual reasons for its performance in a Register Office – because one or both of the parties have been divorced, wholesale family disapproval, haste, financial stress or secrecy.

It might be because of differing faiths between the bride and the bridegroom – irreconcilable but with a mutual agreement not to let either faith encroach upon the other; it could be that the parties have no religious beliefs or simply because their future plans demand the holding of the wedding on a given date and their local church is not available.

In such cases it might well be that the bride and her bridegroom, together with the chief bridesmaid, the best man and the couple's parents arrive at the Register Office dressed in the full regalia of a formal ceremony – bridal gown, veil, morning suits and wedding ties; all prepared to engage in a full-scale wedding reception afterwards.

The wedding itself, of course, will still be restricted to the limitations of the civil law – but both before and afterwards the best man will be required to carry out the full responsibilities of his office.

A Double Wedding, the marriage of two couples at the same service before the same clergyman, at the same time and as part of a single ceremony, is rather uncommon. The usual reason for such an event is the desire of two sisters – or occasionally brothers – to be married at the same time, generally at the behest of their parents. Twin daughters have been inveigled into such a marriage by kindly, but scheming parents – and such an occasion is indeed an event of importance in any community, to be looked forward to with eager delight by friends and neighbours.

Triple weddings occur at less frequent intervals, for similar reasons and creating even more widespread interest – and it is by no means unknown for larger groups to be married in a 'mass' wedding before a vast 'congregation', generally with some political or 'cult' motivation behind it.

The wedding of two or more couples at the same service, may well be and usually is, attended by the full formality and pageantry associated with a 'most important' occasion. Each bridegroom will be support-ed by his own best man, and each of the brides by her quota of bridesmaids. Each best man will undertake precisely the same duties on behalf of 'his' bridegroom as if the wedding was to consist of but a single bridal couple – though he may well find the need for conferences with the other best man – or 'men' – to ensure that the whole affair runs cohesively and in harmony.

Orders of precedence become necessary where double – or multiple – weddings take place and the long-established rules are:

(a) The elder bridegroom is assumed to be the senior – without regard to the possible claims of the supporting families, or to the unlikely objections of one or both of the brides.

(b) In the procession, the brides' father would walk up the centre of the aisle with the senior bride (that is, the daughter who is to marry the elder bridegroom) on his right arm, and the junior bride on his left arm. Each bride would have her own bridesmaid(s) behind her.

Procession for a double wedding of two sisters.

If the brides are not sisters, then each party in the procession should be complete in itself. The bride of the senior bridegroom advances down the aisle on the arm of her father first, followed by her bridesmaids and pages. A few paces behind comes the second bride on *her* father's arm, with her own retinue of bridesmaids.

(c) The senior bridegroom and his bride take their vows first.

(d) The actual positioning of all the participants during the service will vary according to the architecture of the church, the space available, the width of the aisle, and the views and ideas of the clergyman, whose experience of previous double weddings is likely to be extremely limited! The most important thing is that the brides' father gives the right girl to the right man. Adequate rehearsal is essential.

(e) The move to the vestry after the service should be led by the clergyman followed by the senior bridegroom and his bride – and those who are to accompany them there to sign, or witness the signing of the register. The junior bridegroom, his bride and his entourage follow next until both parties are in the vestry.

(f) The senior couple sign the register first, followed by their witnesses. Then follow the junior couple and their witnesses.

The two best men take an opportunity to leave the vestry as soon as possible and make their way as quickly as they can to the church door where they are responsible, jointly, for manoeuvring the two wedding parties, separately and together, before the photographers – and thereafter to their cars.

(g) In the recession each party should again be complete in itself – the senior bridegroom, his bride and their attendants and relatives, lead the way down the aisle and to the church door, separated by only a few paces from the second couple and their supporters.

Each best man should endeavour to see his 'own' bridal couple and their family and friends into their cars *en route* for the reception rooms – but it is quite in order for one to assist the other if it will help to get the cars away quickly, particularly if it is a wet day when the taxis can draw up at the door only one at a time.

Where the duties of the two best men happen to clash, he who is in attendance on the senior bridegroom assumes the right of priority. This position of leadership is normally exercised at the reception where a single receiving line will be enough if the brides (or the bridegrooms) are relatives and are, in consequence, supported by the same parents.

Though it is possible for the two best men to take it in turns to marshal the reception guests past the receiving line, it is not possible for both to reply to the toast 'the bridesmaids' – unless the speeches are to go on interminably and become a series of repetitions. It is usual for the senior best man to undertake this duty – and, perhaps, delegate the post of toastmaster to the junior best man.

This is a matter, however, for the senior best man to decide. He may well feel that his colleague is a better speaker than himself and reverse the accepted procedure.

10

Other Denominations

The Roman Catholic Church

There are two different types of marriage service within the rites of the Roman Catholic faith. The 'Marriage celebrated during Mass' and the 'Marriage celebrated outside Mass'.

The 'Marriage celebrated during Mass' is much more elaborate, though the duties of the best man vary little from that expected in a 'Marriage celebrated outside Mass'. In each ceremony the first part is almost identical. This consists of an Entrance Rite, a Service of The Word, and the Rite of Marriage. Where the Mass is to be celebrated the Liturgy of the Eucharist follows.

Two forms of the Entrance Rite are possible. In the first, the best man and the bridesmaids, along with the groom await the arrival of the bride at the door of the church. The priest greets the bride and groom at the church door, and a procession to the altar follows with the servers and the priest going first, followed by the bride and groom, best man and bridesmaid(s) and the parents. In a more traditional form of entry, the best man is standing at the groom's right hand in the place designated for them, usually the first pew on the right hand side of the church. They await the arrival of the bride, who processes through the church with her father.

The Liturgy of the Word is mainly concerned with up to three readings from the Scriptures, after which the priest may deliver a homily. The Rite of Marriage follows. The arrangements for the marriage ceremony vary from place to place, according to the arrangements of the church furniture. Usually at this stage the bride and groom stand together in front of the priest. The best man stands on the right of the groom; he should make sure that he has the wedding ring, or rings with him. After the exchange of vows and when the priest has said: 'What God has joined together, let no man put asunder', the blessing and exchange of rings follows. The normal custom is for the best man to place the ring(s) on a silver dish where it is blessed by the priest. The husband then places the ring on the wife's finger, and if the husband is to receive a ring, the wife places it on his finger. Bidding prayers follow, after which the couple together with the witnesses sign the Civil Register. This may be done in the church, or in the sacristy. Almost invariably, although it is by no means obligatory, the best man and the chief bridesmaid are appointed by the bridal couple as the official witnesses.

When the Register has been signed, the ceremony either concludes with a final blessing, or the Nuptial Mass may follow. If this is the case, the best man and bridesmaids retire to the pews where they began the ceremony. At the end of the ceremony the recessional begins. The bride moves down the aisle on the arm of her husband, and the best man and chief bridesmaid take their place immediately behind. They should be followed in their turn by the bridesmaids in pairs. Behind them, the father of the bride should escort the bridegroom's mother and the bride's mother should accompany the bridegroom's father. Bringing up the rear, the brothers and sisters of the bridal couple should follow in a similar manner to that of their parents.

On reaching the church door, the best man will assume the mantle of marshal – for the wedding photographs and the departures for the scene of the reception that is to follow.

There are certain other requirements which are no direct concern of the best man, but it is well that he should be aware of them as his advice may be sought.

1. A marriage inside the Mass is permitted in all cases except where one of the parties is not baptized.

2. A marriage between a Catholic and a non-Catholic requires a dispensation from the parish priest.

3. Without a dispensation a marriage between a Catholic and a non-baptized person is invalid.

4. The Catholic party has to undertake to avoid the danger of falling away from the faith, and sincerely to promise to do everything possible to ensure the Catholic baptism and upbringing of all children of the marriage.

5. The priest must be able to sign a statement saying that in his opinion the non-Catholic will not oppose the fulfilment of the promise made by the Catholic.

6. Both parties will usually be asked to attend some form of marriage preparation. This will cover a variety of topics, some of these specifically concerning the essential qualities of Christian marriage, and some more general.

7. The wedding will normally take place in a Catholic church, but for good reasons a dispensation can be granted from this.

Though the duties of the best man during the actual wedding service are minimal, he cannot escape the more arduous tasks that are expected of him both before and after the wedding. The details of these duties vary but little from church to church and can be accepted as standard – except where otherwise stated in this chapter.

Although the marriage of *divorced persons* is normally refused in the Catholic Church, there may be cases where a previous marriage, for some reason, is not recognised by the Church. In these cases a church marriage would normally be permitted. Such cases would exist when a declaration of nullity of the previous marriage had been granted to one of the persons by the Catholic Church, or if a previous marriage had not complied with Church Law, as in the case of a Catholic who had been originally married in a civil Register Office.

In any event, the priest who is to conduct the service should be consulted well in advance by the couple for their own benefit, as if there are any 'snags' to be ironed out, this will give them plenty of time to get them organised. This applies particularly in the case of a 'mixed marriage' where one of the bridal couple is a non-Catholic. In this case, the priest should be consulted several months before the proposed wedding day.

The Free Churches

Though the Free Churches vary considerably in

style, their marriage services are basically similar. They are likely to be simpler than those of the Church of England, but have the same intention and purpose.

A best man needs no special briefing in order to be able to perform his duties satisfactorily – so long as he follows the precepts laid down in this book. Most Free Church ministers like to have a rehearsal of the ceremony, and the presence of the best man is important. His pre-wedding encouragement for the bridegroom, his duties during the service and his leadership during the celebrations afterwards follow the same pattern as is customary where the marriage is to take place within the rites of the Church of England. Many Free Churches do not have a centre aisle so everybody concerned should check which aisle is going to be used by the main participants for entering and leaving the church.

Also, it is a wise precaution to check with the bridal couple the minor details of the service peculiar to their church. The degree of formality varies somewhat from church to church which may be reflected in the celebrations afterwards. For example 'grace' may be said before the wedding breakfast, alcohol may not be served, and speeches may have a more serious tone.

Quakers (Religious Society of Friends)

A Quaker wedding is a most solemn and at the same time a simple service. There is no pageantry, no ceremonial, no attendants, no music and no set sermon. In fact there is no public religious service – and no wedding ring.

The marriage is peculiar to the Society of Friends and consists mainly of silent, corporate worship. There is no preacher, no leader and no set procedure. The gathering is usually held in a Quaker Meeting House, made up of friends, relatives and even strangers. There is seldom a best man or a bridesmaid and the dress is wholly informal.

Only those who feel moved by the Spirit will rise to speak or kneel to pray.

At some point during the meeting the bridegroom and bride take one another's hands and they will rise together, to their feet. Then the bridegroom will make his declaration:

'Friends, I take this my friend .... to be my wife, promising, through Divine assistance, to be unto her a loving and faithful husband so long as we both on earth shall live.'

The bride makes her own declarations in similar terms – then the wedding certificate is signed by the bridal couple in front of the Registering Officer. Two witnesses add their names and then the Registering Officer reads aloud the certificate. Afterwards, it is common practice for all others present at the meeting to append their signatures to the document.

Though there is no official place for the wedding ring during the marriage rites, it is the custom for the couple to exchange rings afterwards.

It is usual at the close of the meeting for worship for the couple to withdraw with full witnesses and the registering officer to complete the civil marriage register.

The Jewish Wedding

The Civil Law requires that all marriages take place

before a Superintendent Registrar of Marriages and where Jews are concerned this marriage can be held in advance of the religious service or takes place at the synagogue straight after the religious service. This is possible where the synagogue's Minister or secretary is recognised as the Registrar's representative by being a Secretary for Marriages.

A marriage under Jewish rites may only take place between two Jews – and they must be able to provide documentation to prove this, such as for example, that their parents were married in accordance with the Jewish rites themselves.

Though it is not absolutely obligatory for the best man to be of the same faith as the bridegroom, it must indeed be a rare occasion when he is not.

Generally, however, the best man is chosen from amongst the bridegroom's brothers, the senior having priority. Failing this, it is quite common for the selection to be made from amongst the bride's brothers. When neither the bridegroom nor his bride have brothers, the best man must perforce be chosen from amongst friends, but even then, it is usual to nominate a relative.

In any event the duties of a best man are almost lost in the assistance given by the male relatives of both the bridegroom and the bride. The bridegroom is even escorted to his place under the canopy, where the wedding is solemnized, by his father, his bride's father and other male relatives of the two families.

The same escort then returns to the door of the synagogue – or wherever the ceremony is taking place – to meet the bride and to conduct her to her place at the side of her betrothed, under the canopy – on his *right*.

The details of the service varies between the orthodox synagogues, the more liberal and the reform communities, but in general the 'advisers' and 'attendants' on the bridegroom should be aware of the following customs and restrictions:

(a) The religious service may take place at any time of the day, on any day of the week, with the exception of Saturday; certain days of festival or mourning are also barred.

(b) On the Sabbath preceding the wedding, the bridal couple, accompanied by the father of each of them, should attend divine service. During the service the bridegroom and close relatives will be honoured by being called upon to read passages from the Scroll of the Law.

(c) The bride wears a veil at her wedding, together with long sleeves and gloves.

Everybody present, including the male members of the party, must have their heads covered.

Etiquette at the Synagogue can vary. However, the groom is always expected to arrive first. Usually he sits in the Warden's box with his father, future father-in-law, and best man.

The groom takes his place first under the *chuppah* (wedding canopy). The best man stands behind and to his left, with the ring handy.

The bride is generally brought in by her father, followed by bridesmaids, bride's mother with escort (or male relative), and bridegroom's parents. According to old Jewish custom, however, the bride is brought in by her mother and future mother-in-law. Both sets of parents usually stand beneath the *chuppah*.

Before the bride comes under the *chuppah*, however, the groom is formally requested by the Minister to approve the appointment of two witnesses of the *ketubah* (Marriage document) and accept the terms and conditions of the *ketubah* whereby he undertakes a number of obligations to his wife.

The bride stands under the *chuppah* at the groom's right. At each side of the *chuppah* stand the *unterfuhrers*, usually the couple's parents.

Next come the blessings of Betrothal, recited over a cup of wine. The first blessing is for wine and the second praises God for commanding us concerning forbidden marriages.

In Jewish law, the couple become married when the man places the ring on the woman's finger, with her acceptance signifying consent. It is important to note that this act effecting their union is carried out by the parties themselves, and it is not the Minister who 'marries' them, but they who marry each other, and the Minister's presence is as an expert in Jewish law, and sometimes as witness to the ketubah as well as in a civil capacity if he is Secretary for Marriages.

Since the ring has such importance, it must be the groom's property; should be of precious metal, but without jewels, and the bride should wear no other ring or jewellery during the ceremony. The ring is placed on the bride's right index finger, but she may transfer it to the 'ring finger' later. The reason for Jewish insistence on a plain ring is to allow no difference between rich and poor, and to avoid any deception or misunderstanding as to its value. It is placed on the right index finger because in ancient transactions this finger was used symbolically to acquire things.

The groom recites in Hebrew a declaration 'Behold, thou art consecrated unto me by this ring according to the law of Moses and of Israel', implying that both parties are properly married in accordance with Jewish law.

The *ketubah* is now read in Aramaic original and in English abstract and handed to the bride. She should look after it carefully since it is her interests which it recognises, and should it be lost she should get it replaced.

Then follow the seven blessings of Marriage, with the final words of prayer that the bride and groom might find the perfect happiness of Adam and Eve and live a life of 'joy and gladness, mirth and exultation, pleasure and delight, love and brotherhood, peace and companionship'. At the conclusion of the Betrothal and the marriage blessings, the couple sip wine to symbolise the fact that they must share the same cup of life whether it be sweet or otherwise. This is followed by the breaking of a glass by the groom.

The ceremony concludes by the Minister pronouncing the blessing, in the heartfelt wish that its words of blessing, protection, grace and peace be fulfilled for bride and groom.

The couple sign the marriage documents, the bride signing her maiden name. The group leave the Synagogue in procession with their attendants. Before greeting their guests at the reception they should spend a few minutes together in private (*yihud*) denoting their newly-acquired status as husband and wife entitled to live together under the same roof.

Civil Marriages

Such marriages are often preferred where religious difficulties or scruples have to be faced. It might be that a religious service has been denied because of the divorce of one or both of the parties; perhaps religious differences between the bride and the bridegroom are irreconcilable; maybe the couple have no religious beliefs and possibly because family disapproval suggests a 'secret' wedding.

Absolute secrecy is, of course, not possible as notice of the intention to marry must be published – usually in the form of a notice at the entrance to the Register Office – but who stops to examine the notice-board? Unless it be a Press reporter on the watch for the 'secret' wedding of some person of interest to the general public.

The civil marriage, performed in a Register Office by a Superintendent Registrar, has no religious connotations. Nor are religious beliefs, practices or scruples taken into account when applications for civil marriages are examined by the Registrar.

Nor may a Registrar refuse to perform a marriage because of divorce, colour or creed – nor may he refuse his services for any other reason, provided that the couple concerned are eligible and have complied with the Civil Law.

He needs to know only:

(a) That both participants in the marriage are 18 years of age – or being 16, have the written consent of their parents.

(b) Application must be made in the district where the couple wish to marry. The couple should have resided in that district for not less than seven days – or, if only one lives in that locality, the Registrar will inform the Superintendent Registrar of the district in which the other resides. Where parties reside in different registration districts notice must be given in *each* district.

(c) They are not within the prohibited degree of relationship to one another as listed in the Book of Common Prayer.

(d) If either party has been married previously, he or she must produce to the Superintendent Registrar either a certificate of death of the previous spouse, or in the event of a divorce, the decree absolute.

(e) If the parents have refused consent to the marriage of a son or daughter under the age of 18, the couple being not less than 16 years of age, may apply to the courts for permission. If the magistrates consider their plea justified, they may reverse the decision of the parents and grant their consent.

(f) Three weeks' notice is required by the Superintendent Registrar – though it is possible to obtain a Superintendent's Licence by application to the Registrar whereby the marriage requires only one clear working day's notice.

In Scotland the age of consent is 16 – at which age consent is the sole prerogative of the couple concerned – and requires no confirmation from their parents or guardians.

The details of the brief – but fully binding – service and the duties of the best man in connection with such a marriage have been given on page 64, and require no repetition.

11

The Reception

The parents of the bride are the hosts at the reception following the wedding ceremony. It is they who decide whether to have the reception at home, in a marquee in the garden, in a suitable local hall or at a local hotel. They will decide on the menu and the wines, order the wedding cake, arrange for the decorations and any other facilities such as a changing room for the bride.

It is they who send out the invitations – after consulting the bridegroom concerning his wishes in the matter; but as it is the bride's parents who will have the bill to pay, it is they who must be allowed to decide the scale of the reception; the numbers to be invited and the quality and style of the meal.

No doubt the bride will be permitted a good deal of say in the matter – though she may well find herself faced with the parental ultimatum of 'A real slap up wedding with a token wedding present – or a less pretentious affair and a substantial gift towards your new home. It's up to you!'

Whatever the decision, the best man will be anxious for details in order that he can make his own arrangements for the event. He will be particularly anxious to know, for instance:

(a) The premises where the reception is to be held – and the facilities it will afford, such as changing rooms and the spot where the receiving line can most conveniently be established.

(b) The number of guests to be expected with special reference to any V.I.P.s who may be expected to attend.

(c) The expected time of arrival of the guests – and the bridal couple.

(d) If photographs are to be taken in the reception rooms – before the reception, during it, and the cutting of the cake.

(e) The time set for the meal. (Is it hot or cold? Obviously promptness is of importance. Essential if it is to be a hot meal.)

(f) Arrangements made for the receipt of telemessages and where they can be collected – if the caterer is not to place them on the table beside the wedding cake.

(g) The seating plan – if there is to be one – and where it is to be shown for the convenience of guests.

(h) Who are the speakers to be. This is chiefly a matter for the best man, but he should make careful enquiries to ensure that there are no duplications, not too many of them (the bridal couple will have a departure time to keep to) and that speakers will not rise until they are called upon.

(i) The time the couple must depart to catch their plane (or train, or ferry) for the start of their honeymoon.

And he will want to know who, after the departure of the newly-weds and their guests:

(i) will be expected to collect the remains of the wedding cake and take it to the home of the bride's mother, and

(ii) who is to be responsible for gathering together, packing and transporting to the home of the bride's mother, the collection of wedding presents if they have been on display.

It is quite usual today for a reception to be held at the home of the bride's parents. Generally, the modern house has neither the space nor the kitchen facilities to cope with meals for more than a very limited number of guests. A popular solution is to hire a marquee to put in the garden, often connected to the house by an awning (in case of rain), and to engage the services of a caterer, who will prepare a meal, serve it and the drinks and

The marquee is a popular solution.

clear up at the end of the day, thus saving the bride's parents a great deal of extra worry. These modern marquees come in various widths and can be made up in any length. They can have coloured linings, wood floors, platforms, dance floors and matting to cover them, and can include chandeliers, spot and flood lighting if required. These firms provide a large range of chairs and tables, from the elegant to the functional and will also provide heaters according to the season.

If the bride's parents decide on a marquee, they will often use it to hold a dance or disco for the newly-weds and their younger guests, who may not have been invited to the reception, during the evening.

There are many firms available today that specialise in such functions and supplying accommodation and meals to suit all purposes – and purses. A hotel is often ideal – it can provide changing rooms for the bride and, if required, for the bridegroom, reception facilities apart from the restaurant and probably a separate room for the display of the wedding presents if required.

Banqueting halls often provide similar amenities and, of course, there are smaller premises such as village halls which are perfectly adequate for smaller receptions.

The bridal couple usually stand outside the church for their wedding photographs to be taken. These can take fifteen minutes or more, depending on the number of relatives and friends who are to be included in them, and they may also take some more photographs by their wedding car before leaving for the reception. They will be followed by their parents, and then by the best man, who will bring the bridesmaids in his car. In the few minutes before the guests arrive it is usual for the formal photographs of the cutting of the cake to be taken by the official photographer. As the caterer may

The reception line.

remove one tier to start cutting it up, this may be the
only time to get a photograph of the complete cake.
The principals will then normally form a reception line
to receive the guests. The guests will first meet the
bride's mother and father (as the hosts), followed by
the bridegroom's parents and then the bride and
bridegroom. Alternatively, it can be the bride's
parents, followed by bride and groom, followed by
bridegroom's parents. The bridesmaids will stand at
the end of the line to greet the guests.

The best man can direct the guests towards the bride's parents himself, or in some cases, there may be a Master of Ceremonies who will ask the guests' names and announce them before they go in to meet their hosts officially. The ushers should help to marshal the guests on their way to the receiving line.

The bride should never be congratulated on her marriage; she should be offered best wishes for her happiness!

The best man will need to encourage the guests to move on past the reception line as quickly as possible otherwise there is likely to be considerable delay, if fulsome guests are allowed to 'gush' over the newly-weds. This is most important at larger weddings otherwise the queue of guests can become long and could even stretch outside into the rain!

The best man should keep an eye on the time so that everything runs smoothly and without haste right up to the departure of the bride and bridegroom (which should be at a pre-arranged time). They will, of course, want to talk to their guests and this is much easier to do during a buffet reception than at the end of a more formal, sit-down meal, when there is little time left before leaving the reception.

Having passed along the reception line the guests will then be offered a drink – sparkling wine, sherry, champagne, apple juice or grape juice and there will be nuts and other titbits to nibble.

At very formal receptions, a toast-master will call the guests to their seats. Otherwise, it is more usual for the bride and groom, having received their guests, to approach the buffet tables in order to be served first, which is the signal for others to follow.

At a reception given in a marquee at the bride's home the menu could be a cold buffet and include such items as plaice in orange sauce with anchovies, crab mayonnaise, chicken with grapes and almonds, roast fillet of beef, gammon with pineapple, avocado mousse, terrine of duck with bacon, or salmon and cucumber flan served with a large variety of salads followed by a choice of exotic sweets. All these items can be specially prepared as fork buffet food so that the bride and groom can circulate among friends and relatives, and they too can move around instead of being confined to one place. A good host will make certain that there are enough chairs and tables so that every guest can sit if they wish to.

There is no longer any need to feel that the only food that can be safely offered at a 'stand-up' reception is canapes, vol-au-vent, bridge rolls, etc. Caterers will now offer a menu to suit all tastes and purses.

If the Wedding Breakfast is to be a sit-down meal, or is taking place in a hotel there should be a large seating plan near the door for the convenience of the guests, but the best man should have a general idea of the arrangements in advance. He should, in any event, know the exact placings at the top table.

As soon as the majority have begun to find their seats, the best man would be well advised to show the bridesmaids to their places and leave the still-waiting guests to be guided by the ushers.

Seating arrangements are very much a matter for the hostess, with the advice of the caterer, although she almost invariably consults her daughter who in turn seeks the advice of the bridegroom who probably asks the best man for his ideas on the subject.

The number of guests to be seated at the top table depends largely on the total number who are to be invited, and on the shape and layout of the room concerned.

As it is usual for the bride and bridegroom to be seated together in the middle of this table, it must seat an even number of people. And only one side of the table should have places – so that the bridal couple may have an unimpeded view of their guests, and more important, the guests be able to see the principals.

A typical seating layout.

The most common method of arranging a top table is that shown on page 88 but other suggestions such as those contained below and on page 90 are sometimes preferred and are equally acceptable.

An alternative seating layout.

As soon as the guests have found their seats, the bridal couple should move towards their places at the top table, together. They should be followed by:

Another possibility.

The bride's father with the bridegroom's mother.

The bridegroom's father with the bride's mother.

The best man with the chief bridesmaid.

The bridesmaids.

The pages.

When everyone is seated the best man should obtain silence and if 'grace' is to be said, call upon the clergyman or minister present to 'say grace'. Often, in the absence of a clergyman or minister, a known member of a church among the guests may be invited to 'say grace'. But he or she should be approached in advance. Failing any of these arrangements the duty should be undertaken by the bride's father. One of the following forms of words would be suitable:

(a) For our families, our friends and for this food which you give us, we thank you Lord.

(b) Receive our thanks, O Lord, for this food and for this happy day.

(c) We thank you, our Father, for good food which brings health, and human love which brings happiness.

(d) For what we are about to receive, may the Lord make us truly thankful and ever mindful of the needs of others.

Grace is often neglected nowadays, but should never be omitted if a minister of religion is present.

When the coffee stage is reached, the best man should call for order and then introduce the first speaker. It is normally the bride's father whom he should call on to propose the toast of 'the health and happiness of the bride and bridegroom', but it is by no means uncommon for this duty to be passed to some other male member of the bride's family who is perhaps a better speaker or who happens to be someone of importance.

This duty should never, however, be passed on without the consent of the bride's father; he has a vested interest in the passing of his daughter from the shelter of his home to the care of another, and may wish to say so. In fact, the delegation of this 'right' is usual only where it is the express wish of the bride's father that another should make the speech.

Care should be taken, too, to ensure that no-one is expected to deputize for the bride's father without due warning; even the best of speakers expect some time in which to gather together the material for their speeches.

The bridegroom replies on behalf of himself and his bride, taking the opportunity to thank his parents for their love and care during his boyhood, for the start they have given him in life – and for their good wishes for his future and that of his wife. The groom also takes this opportunity on 'behalf of his wife and himself' to thank all those present for their gifts, and to invite them to come and see them in their new home.

Should there be any close members of the family who have not come to the wedding because of illness or other reasons, he should say how sorry he and his wife are that they are not present and to wish them a speedy recovery.

From this serious note, the bridegroom should now switch to a lighter note as he proposes the toast of 'the bridesmaids', and thank them for a job well done.

It is the best man's duty to respond to this toast on behalf of the bridesmaids. His speech should be light in character and designed to bring an air of joy to the occasion – a mood that should persist from that moment on, right through the proceedings. His speech should be the 'high-spot' of the reception and it is very often his ability to make this particular speech, with humour and interest, that is the deciding consideration in his selection as best man. (See Chapter 14 for speeches.)

Those are the three accepted speeches usual to a wedding reception. No further speeches are required and as often as not, none are given.

Other speeches are, however, permissible; it is not unusual for the bridegroom's father to thank the host and hostess for the occasion and for the bride's father to reply – very briefly if he has already spoken.

Others may wish to speak but the best man must keep a wary eye on the clock.

A few suggestions for speeches are offered in Chapter 14, but they should only be used as a skeleton into which the speaker can introduce the personalities, the incidents and the jokes that will be understood by his audience.

As soon as the best man judges that the speeches have run their course, or that it is time to bring them to an end, he should rise to his feet to read the telemessages of congratulations and good wishes addressed to the bridal pair from their absent friends and relations.

In reading these aloud to the assembled guests, the best man should do his best to add a few pithy comments concerning the contents and perhaps a few light references to the senders. If this is not done, boredom may depress the guests, particularly if there are a lot of telemessages and a number of them have been sent by people unknown to the audience as a whole. In the event of receiving a large number of good luck messages, the best man can always list them together by saying 'N and M have also received best wishes from Auntie Vi in Australia, Robert, Sarah and Joanne in Texas, Emma and Michael in Aberdeen' and so on, keeping the original and humorous messages until the end. In order to keep the whole thing amusing it has been known for best men to insert some pseudo messages such as:

From your bank manager: Keep up the interest rate.

From your stockbroker: Share and share alike for the best dividends.

From your doctor: Don't be an anti-body now.

From the groom's secretary: You're not the boss now.

After the reception – or more usually – after the honeymoon, the bridegroom must see to it that these telemessages are passed to the bride. The safest place to lodge them is with the bride's mother – but it is the bride's duty to acknowledge them on her return from the honeymoon, usually at the same time as she writes to thank those who have sent her and her husband wedding gifts.

There is no delay between the reading of the telemessages and the cutting of the wedding cake. The best man merely indicates to the bridal couple that the time for this happy custom has arrived.

The bridegroom should lead his bride to the most convenient place beside the cake – usually on the opposite side of the table to where they have been sitting. The caterer or one of his staff will be in attendance and he will assist the bride to place the point of the knife in the proper place near the middle of the bottom tier of the cake – and with the cutting edge towards her.

The bridegroom should then place his hand over that of his wife and slowly and carefully help her to push the point of the blade into the heart of the cake and then to

Cutting the cake.

draw it forward and downwards in a slicing movement.

That usually completes the token 'cutting of the cake'. The bride and her groom are not expected to undertake the laborious task of dividing the cake; this is a task to be undertaken by the caterer who will also pass the portions around on plates, sometimes with the assistance of the bridesmaids.

It is the caterer's job to dismantle the cake as he cuts it and set aside a considerable portion from which the bride, or her mother, will send small boxed portions to those of their friends, relatives and acquaintances who have been unable to attend the wedding and the reception afterwards.

It used to be traditional for the bridesmaids to keep their slices of cake and to place them under their pillows that night – in the belief that they will dream of their own future husbands; the best man warning them of the disastrous consequences that might overtake them if they happen to dream of some other man than their current boyfriends!

The reception proper is now over. It is time for the bride to retire with her chief bridesmaid to change from her wedding finery into her 'going away' clothes.

Traditionally, as she climbs the stairs to her changing room, her bridesmaids gather at the foot – or if there are no stairs, around the doorway through which she will pass to prepare for her departure.

The bride throws her bouquet.

Everybody else should assemble behind the brides-maids to watch as the bride throws her bouquet towards the bridesmaids. The young lady who captures the floral tribute is said, reputedly, to be the next bride. Nowadays the bride often throws her bouquet as she and her husband get into the car to leave for their honeymoon.

At this stage the best man should accompany the bridegroom to wherever he is to change for his honeymoon journey. If he has a changing room in the same building the matter is a relatively simple affair, but if he has to rush home to change, there is no time to be wasted. He must be ready and waiting in the reception room when his wife returns, all ready to leave. If they are to leave by car for their destination, the luggage of the bride and groom will normally have been loaded in advance. If they are to depart by taxi, the baggage should be assembled by the exit.

As soon as the bridegroom has changed, the best man should check and hand over to him all the necessary documents required for the honeymoon; rail, ferry or air tickets; passports, inoculation certificates, travellers' cheques, hotel reservations, time-tables – and the marriage certificate if the bride has not already got it.

The departure of the bride and the bridegroom should not be delayed if emotional scenes are to be avoided. The days of long separation between a bride and her mother are almost a thing of the past. The speed of modern communications; the telephone and high-speed travel make the parting much less 'final' than it used to be.

While the newly-weds are saying their 'goodbyes' to their parents – and this is the time when the groom may join in a growing custom of presenting the bride's mother and his own mother with a bouquet of flowers to thank them for all they have done to make the day so happy and memorable – the best man and the ushers should be making quite sure that the honeymoon luggage is loaded aboard their transport, that coats have not been forgotten, handbags overlooked – and that they are still in time to catch their plane.

While the last of the farewells are being exchanged, briskly and cheerfully, let us hope, the younger ushers and bridesmaids will probably be tying old shoes and 'Just Married' notices on to the back of the honeymoon car, a delight rarely omitted – though the 'jokers' will no doubt be well aware that the bridegroom will stop the car as soon as it rounds the first corner to remove the tokens.

Not until the bridal couple have finally departed should the guests begin to leave. As they go they should

They have all gone.

say their farewells to their hosts, the parents of the bride, followed by a parting word with the parents of the bridegroom – until only they, the best man and the ushers, and the chief bridesmaid and her bridesmaids and pages remain.

12

And Afterwards

It is becoming more common in these days of long
distance travel that an evening entertainment is
arranged. If relatives have come from afar, or the
groom's parents are staying overnight in a nearby
hotel, it is customary for the two sets of parents and any
other relatives and friends to get together and either
have an informal party at the bride's parents' home or
go out to dinner, which will dispel any feeling of anti-
climax after the newly-weds have left for their
honeymoon.

As mentioned earlier, many bridal couples stay on
and invite young friends, who perhaps were not present
at the main reception, to an evening disco. There are no
pretensions or niceties here. The music is loud and beer
is drunk.

The best man would not leave until all the
celebrations were over and he could no longer find any
task needing his attention. If the gifts have been on
display he may be asked to help pack them away and
transport them to the newly-weds' home. He may also
be expected to see the bridesmaids home.

It may be that the remains of the wedding cake need
to be carefully packed and transported to the bride's
parents' home, too. Her mother may wish to box and

post portions of it to friends and relatives who were unable to attend the wedding – though it is quite in order for this task to be delayed until the bridal couple return from their honeymoon.

The bride's mother will undoubtedly gather together her daughter's wedding finery from the changing room, but the best man will need to perform the same service for the bridegroom.

Before finally leaving the reception rooms, the best man should make a search to make sure that nothing has been left behind by the bridal couple, or the guests.

Coats, umbrellas, gloves and so on should be taken to the home of the bride's mother. It is there that the forgetful guests will call when they miss their belongings.

The best man also has to remember to pack the hired garments for himself and the groom, and return them to the hirers.

13

Anniversaries

Anniversaries of a wedding are almost always a matter of remembrance between the man and his wife – and too often forgotten by everyone else. Even the couple themselves soon find themselves treating the annual event more casually. Perhaps an exchange of gifts, maybe a night out – and very often a mere 'happy anniversary' wish is the only 'celebration'.

Of course, as the years go by, the responsibilities of a growing family tend to detract from the interest of 'fading' memories. Schooling, mumps, children's birthdays, holidays, and in due course children's engagements and weddings! Grandchildren, more mumps, more birthdays ...

However, it is the custom – though much honoured in the breach today – for the best man to remind the couple of their anniversaries with an 'anniversary' card, or perhaps a floral tribute. Nothing more is required as any celebrations are accepted as the private affair of the couple – and the best man may only expect, if his memento is more than a card, no more than a cheerful acknowledgement.

After a very few years, even this small reminder by the best man is inclined to lapse. Probably he too has married and is becoming deeply embroiled in the ties of a growing family of his own. School holidays, children's Christmas parties, measles . . .

But as long as he remains single, a best man should not altogether forget his friend's anniversary. Even if it becomes no more than a telephone call, his wife at least will appreciate the thought.

And still the years gather dust – until the best man is faced with an invitation to his friend's Silver Wedding party! Probably only then does he realise that twenty-five long years have gone by since he stood at his friend's side, facing the altar.

It is the 'bridal couple's' duty to send out the invitations for this anniversary party. A service in the church where they were married may start the day, but more often than not the urge is to celebrate with a small party.

A dinner party, perhaps followed by a visit to a theatre or a night-club or a dance, may be the order of the day. But whatever it is, the scale and scope of the party will rest with the couple, whose financial situation and the number of their family may dictate the venue and the type of entertainment they offer.

The invitations will normally include:

Sons and daughters.

Wives and husbands of the above.

Best man, and assuming she has become a good friend his wife.

Chief bridesmaid and her husband.

The officiating clergyman at their wedding, perhaps.

The 'bride's' parents.

The 'bridegroom's' parents.

Guests at the wedding who are or have become very close friends. The numbers depending on the total number of the party.

After twenty-five years there are likely to be many gaps in the above list. Parents may have passed on, others may now live far away – and some whose present addresses have been forgotten, will be lost in the mists of time.

Formal wear is only preferred where the couple are in a substantial position in life, in which event it should be copied by all the guests – and guests must be prepared, by asking when the invitations are accepted. Of course, if the invitations are in writing, no doubt this item will be mentioned on the card.

Informality is more usual today even though the party may be held in a restaurant or hotel.

A wedding cake – small – should be on the table, but as it is not the custom to send portions to absent friends, none of it need be saved. In due course it should be cut in the same token fashion as on the occasion of the original wedding reception, twenty-five years ago.

Speeches are usually few and happy. The first is normally made by the couple's eldest son in the form of a toast to their 'continued happiness'. The husband is expected to reply on behalf of his wife and himself.

Where there is no son, the best man proposes the toast.

If there does happen to be a son, the best man is expected to make a speech following that of the husband. This should be full of cheerful reminiscences, probably new to the sons and daughters of the couple – and perhaps a few amusing comparisons between the way of life today and as it was lived a quarter of a century ago.

Silver wedding gifts are given as convenient; some before the party and others as the guests arrive. They should all be of silver, or where that is not feasible because of cost, particularly in the case of presents from young children, they should be tied up with silver ribbon.

In any event, silver is acceptable in the form of silver 'plate', and should not therefore be an embarrassment to impecunious guests.

The party may go on elsewhere after the dinner, though it is quite usual for the younger guests to leave the elders to their cigars and reminiscences.

And with a host of cheerful promises not to forget one another in future and perhaps to meet more often, the party drifts to a conclusion.

But again the years soon fog the promises. Old age begins to restrict the interests of the couple and the barely remembered attendants at their wedding; grandchildren are growing up by now, friends are becoming fewer and memories less clear cut. And almost before you know it the couple's Golden Wedding has come around; fifty years of married life lie behind them.

It is customary for the eldest son – or daughter – to organise a small party to celebrate their parents' Golden Wedding. The guests will comprise the couple's family; sons, daughters, their wives and husbands, grandchildren, probably wih their wives and husbands – and as guests of honour, if they still survive and are available, the best man and the chief bridesmaid who were in attendance at that so long ago wedding.

The announcement of the Golden Wedding will probably be made in the Press and no doubt the best man will receive his invitation to the party either by letter or by telephone.

The party will probably be held in one of the

children's homes or some hotel or restaurant – without formality. There should be a wedding cake of only sufficient size for the purpose, and in due time the bridal couple will cut it as they did the original cake fifty years ago.

This time the presents should be of 'gold', though very often they are much less valuable and merely consist of token gifts tied with 'gold' ribbon. This is particularly apt where the presents are from young great-grandchildren. As the elderly couple either possess, or no longer require gifts of intrinsic value, flowers tied with a ribbon of 'gold' are an ideal tribute from the best man and the chief bridesmaid; the family will have discussed and sorted out any needs the couple may have and contributed accordingly.

Speeches are not essential – except for perhaps a toast to the 'happy couple', and any reply from the bridegroom is usually made from his seat without rising to his feet.

This speech generally drifts into reminiscences and round-the-table conversation – until the eldest son, or a senior member of the couple's family considers that his elderly parents have had enough and are beginning to tire.

Farewells should be said at the table, leaving only perhaps the eldest son and his wife to escort the 'old folks' home.

The best man should undertake to see the chief bridesmaid to her home – if she is not to be collected by a husband of her own, a son – or perhaps even a grandson.

The last, or almost certainly the last, duty of a best man is to attend the Diamond Wedding of the same couple – if they and he have survived the sixty years that have fled by since the first wedding. The party will be small and similar to that held in celebration of their

The Golden Wedding.

Golden Wedding, though the little party may well be held in the home of the aged couple rather than expose them to the fuss and bother of having to be escorted home after they have become over-tired.

Presents rarely include diamonds; for one thing, it can be assumed that valuable gifts are no longer of very great moment to their recipients, and flowers are by far the most suitable of gifts.

The party will be geared by the couple's family so that they are not worried by the health of their parents because of excitement. They have to consider, too, the age of the honoured guests – if they are present. Both the best man and the chief bridesmaid are by now probably in their eighties. So, when some members of the bridal couple's family escort their elderly relatives home, it is expected that some of the younger members will perform the same service for both the best man and the chief bridesmaid.

It must be rare indeed for the ultimate wedding celebration to be attended by the best man and the chief bridesmaid. In fact, as this second 'Diamond Wedding' is the seventy-fifth anniversary of the wedding, it must be equally rare for all the parties to both survive and be available – and physically capable of having a get-together.

Nevertheless, the author of this book wishes, with all sincerity, that the best man who scans these pages, will celebrate the climax of his duties at such an occasion.

Though there is little need to list all the traditional wedding anniversaries, almost forgotten and generally ignored by people today, here again are those of importance which will in all probability be remembered by the bride – and should not be overlooked by the best man:

25th anniversary – the 'Silver Wedding'.

50th anniversary – the 'Golden Wedding'.

60th anniversary – the 'Diamond Wedding'.

75th anniversary – the second 'Diamond Wedding'.

14

Speeches

The best man can look forward to having to make two speeches in support of the bridegroom – that at his stag party and the second at the reception after the wedding when he replies to the toast of 'the bridesmaids'.

The second is, of course, much the more important of the two. It will have to be made to an audience consisting of the bride and bridegroom, the official attendants, the newly-weds' parents and the concourse of guests.

The first is the simpler of the two. It will be given to a limited number of listeners; all of them male, all of them of the same age group and, no doubt, all of them friends of, and well-known to, the best man.

The main speech offered at a stag party is usually made by the best man and is designed both to wish the bridegroom well in his forthcoming marriage and to deplore his departure from the ranks of his bachelor friends and, with tongue in cheek, to warn him of the perils he faces on the tidal waves of the deep sea of matrimony.

The best man should realise, when preparing his speech, that it must be light and amusing. The stag party is traditionally a high-spirited affair and by the time the best man is due to rise to his feet, the guests will 'have wine taken'! For this reason, too, the guests at the party will be talkative and reluctant to spend too much time listening to someone else monopolising the conversation – however witty he may be. In other words he must be brief.

A speech that might by typical of what is expected, could start:

'It is a sad, sad occasion when a man decides to desert the friends of his youth and surrender himself to the machinations of a female. Yet here tonight we are witness to one who has the cheek to bribe us with a meal and a bottle of wine, not to forget him after he has gone, and to offer up unending prayers for his salvation.

'My friends, look at him sitting there at the head of the table, bleary eyed and without a thought for the bevy of weeping beauties I passed on the doorstep as I came in tonight – abandoned, betrayed and broken-hearted. Is his bride aware of these luckless hussies? Or are these cigars the price of our silence? But let us not despise the weakling too deeply. Let us remember, what he appears to have overlooked, that the down-payment on a bride is as nothing to the upkeep thereafter. She will require two pairs of shoes to his one, a dozen pairs of tights to his couple of pairs of socks and a choice of fifty dresses and skirts whilst he travels to town in the same old suit.

'And is that the full tale of financial ruin? Not on your life; just as he decides that he must seek additional employment in the evenings to keep pace with his debts, she will present him with a wailing demander of milk, nappies and transport.

'However, I have good news for him. His friends will remember him with sympathy as they imbibe their accustomed pints at the local on a Saturday night. Indeed, we shall drink an extra at the very thought of him having to stay at home to wash the dishes, repair the drains and probably paper the walls. We shall weep into this extra glass of beer – at the thought that he is not there to pay for it.

'Of course, he knows full well that despite these sombre warnings, we do wish him well for the future – but if he should want to escape it, let him know that we are prepared to have a whip round for loot with which to feed his gas meter; or if he should think enough of his friends to want to spare them the dreary trail behind a hearse, they will gladly cut a hole in the ice on the duck pond, large enough for him to slip through.

'If even these escape routes fail to appeal to him, let us, as a last resort, wish him all the joys of a softer shoulder on which to cry, warmed slippers of an evening by his chair, no more buttonless shirts, a full half share in his own car – and no more need for chilly goodbyes on the girlfriend's doorstep. Lift your glasses everybody and let's sing 'For he's a jolly good fellow.''

The only other obligatory speech of the evening should be the reply from the bridegroom – equally light, amusing and – brief.

There are three customary speeches at the reception following the wedding, though only the time available need restrict others from speaking. These are:

1. From the bride's father who proposes the toast of 'The happiness and prosperity of the bride and bridegroom'.

2. The reply from the bridegroom following which he proposes 'The health and happiness of the bridesmaids'.

3. The best man replies on behalf of the bridesmaids.

Only the third of these directly concerns the best man, but as he may be asked by others for a few hints concerning their own speeches, it will not be out of place here to list some of the thoughts that should be expressed by them.

Where the bride's father proposes the toast to the bridal couple, he should make reference to:

(a) The joy he and his wife have had in the bringing up of their daughter (including a couple of happy incidents of her childhood), and how sadly they will miss her from their home.

(b) The pleasure they have found in getting to know their new son-in-law – and his parents.

(c) The certainty they feel that in her husband's care, their daughter will prosper along with him – and with a little homily on the 'give and take' necessary to a successful marriage – the confidence they have that happiness must accompany the love they so evidently bear for one another.

The bridegroom's reply on behalf of his wife and himself should include:

(a) His gratitude for the care and love he has had at the hands of his parents since he could remember. (Including one or two memories of the happy days he has experienced in his boyhood and youth.)

(b) His gratitude for the start they have given him for his new life. His education, his training towards a livelihood – and where applicable, for the gifts he has received from them and everyone else towards setting up his new home.

(c) He should express his gratitude, on behalf of his wife and himself, for the good wishes with which her father has blessed them. (Probably bringing out the old adage of 'Not having lost a daughter, but gained a son'.)

At this point the bridegroom should switch to a brighter theme with the toast of 'the bridesmaids'.

(d) He may congratulate them on getting his bride to the wedding on time.
(e) He might remark on their good looks and happy demeanour – and their prospects of being inundated with 'male' admirers and the inevitable result.

He can interrupt his speech to give each of the bridesmaids in turn a small gift, going from one to the other to do so, though often if they are presented with lockets, these are given beforehand and worn for the wedding. Then returning to his bride, he should conclude with:

(f) The toast, 'the bridesmaids'.

It is the best man's duty to reply on behalf of the bridesmaids. His speech should be free of all solemnity and designed to add to the note of light entertainment introduced by the bridegroom.

The only way of achieving an apparently effortless and amusing speech is by putting a great deal of effort into its preparation. If he puts off thinking about it until the evening before the wedding, it is unlikely to be a spectacular success! If the result is to be a success, it needs proper planning.

As soon as he is asked to be best man, he should start jotting down amusing and apt stories about weddings, any incidents he remembers or has been told about the bridegroom in his youth, or more recently. Note down some of the triumphs in the bridegroom's life –

orting, academic or career. How did the couple
eet? Is there a story there? Is the bride a very
ganised person, the opposite of the groom; is the
oom a better cook than his wife-to-be. All these
ings are possible sources of ideas for the speech.
hen he has several pages of notes he can start to write
s speech. It should have a beginning, a middle and an
d.

The beginning should be amusing, and arresting
ough to capture his audience's attention and will
obably deal with the bride and groom's triumphs,
hievements and antics.

The middle will include the goodwill and best wishes
om their friends and relatives, how suited they are
d the changes likely to take place in the habits of the
oom – such as washing up every day instead of once a
onth. The best man can also warn the bride in a
king way of any particular idiosyncracies that her
usband has such as being allergic to morning, or
ork, or alarm clocks.

The end of the speech should be a message of hope
r the future, presented as a quotation if a suitable one
n be found.

Having written it out he will probably find it is far
o long and will then have to start pruning it.

It is always a good idea to read it aloud – he can then
ar which bits can be cut out, and if he does it in front
a mirror it should remind him not to look too serious
r to pull faces. If he finds it difficult to memorise the
hole speech, rather than reading it out which will
und rather stilted, he can use a postcard and write
own the main headings, with words that will jog his
emory about a particular story or idea to be included.
ake sure that all notes are in large print so that each
em can be picked out without having to search
rough them.

The Best Man can write down the main headings on a post-card

If he is still not sure about his speech, he should try
out on a friend, and be sure to speak slowly and clearly
It is always better to be brief than to ramble o
endlessly.

He might write:

'I have known, to my cost (the bridegroom) for a ver
long time and though I have not had the pleasure o
knowing (the bride) for so long, I am sure that the
happiness is certain. My only regret is that it wasn't
who met (the bride) first – or at any rate in sufficie
time to warn her of (the bridegroom's) infidelities – o

any other lie I could think up to divert her attentions – elsewhere.

'Here, yet again, is an example of the luck some men get – whether they deserve it or not and of what some girls will fall for! Whilst others of us ...

'I can assure (the bride) of (the bridegroom's) devotion; I have had the most trying time today getting him ready for his wedding. Not because of any reluctance on his part, but because of the times I have had to answer such questions as 'Do you think she'll change her mind at the last minute?' or 'Do you think some clown will dream up a, what do you call it – an impediment when the parson pops the question?' or even such questions as 'Are we going to be late?' and 'Have you forgotten the ring?'

'As if my thoughts weren't already heavily engaged with my duties to the bridesmaids! If, for instance, the best man is allowed to kiss the bride, is he also allowed to kiss the bridesmaids? A wishful thought perhaps – but one that is inclined to distract attention from the less attractive job of seeing that the bridegroom has braced his trousers up to the correct height and cleaned his shoes first.

'If you will glance at the bridesmaids you will understand why I accepted the duties of a best man. Who could possibly deny themselves the opportunity of being associated with them – and who will forget in a very long time their beauty, vivaciousness – and their twinkling eyes?

'In thanking you all for your good wishes on their behalf, I can promise you that you will soon have an opportunity to speak to them personally as they hand round portions of the wedding cake.

He might write himself notes on this speech as follows:

HOW LONG I'VE KNOWN ...

PITY I DIDN'T MEET HIS WIFE FIRST

STORY ABOUT

BRIDEGROOM'S DEVOTION – WILL SHE COME?

WHAT IMPEDIMENT COULD THERE BE?

RING – FIFTY TIMES

CAN I KISS BRIDESMAIDS AND BRIDE? RATHER THAN CLEAN (THE BRIDEGROOM'S) SHOES?

THANKS FOR GOOD WISHES TO BRIDES-MAIDS

Other speeches may follow, but none are obligatory. If time permits toasts may be offered to:

(a) The health of the bridegroom's parents.
(b) The health of the bride's parents.
(c) The health of the minister, if he is present.

But none of these should be allowed to hold up the next item in the reception – the opening and reading of the telemessages followed by the cutting of the cake.

The build-up of each speech should reflect the mood of the reception and the character of him who makes it, but it should be remembered that a wedding is very much a family occasion and wider issues should not be introduced – even where the marriage is a public affair.

Be brief. Many of the family and guests may not have met for a very long time and want to talk about their

ves between. Many still want the chance of a word
ith the newly-weds before they have to rush off on
heir honeymoon journey. And the bride herself needs
me to change into her 'going away' outfit.

Index

Companion volume:

SAMPLE SOCIAL SPEECHES

WIT, STORIES, JOKES, ANECDOTES, EPIGRAMS, Etc.

Gordon Williams

At last!

The book the world has waited for.

Gordon Williams, brilliant British speaker, has worked out a technique based on numerous specimen speeches, to enable *you* to use them to build up your social speech.

He has given you many samples on which you can base a fresh new talk or speech of your own. You can add to it with gay or serious stories from his unique selection, or "salt" it with one or more of his jokes, epigrams and witticisms.

In this new edition, special attention is given to sample speeches suitable for the best man and for others involved with weddings.

Uniform with this volume

ELLIOT RIGHT WAY BOOKS KINGSWOOD, SURREY, U.K.

OUR PUBLISHING POLICY

HOW WE CHOOSE

Our policy is to consider every deserving manuscript and we can give special editorial help where an author is an authority on his subject but an inexperienced writer. We are rigorously selective in the choice of books we publish. We set the highest standards of editorial quality and accuracy. This means that a *Paperfront* is easy to understand and delightful to read. Where illustrations are necessary to convey points of detail, these are drawn up by a subject specialist artist from our panel.

HOW WE KEEP PRICES LOW

We aim for the big seller. This enables us to order enormous print runs and achieve the lowest price for you. Unfortunately, this means that you will not find in the *Paperfront* list any titles on obscure subjects of minority interest only. These could not be printed in large enough quantities to be sold for the low price at which we offer this series. We sell almost all our *Paperfronts* at the same unit price. This saves a lot of fiddling about in our clerical departments and helps us to give you world-beating value. Under this system, the longest titles are offered at a price which we believe to be unmatched by any publisher in the world.

OUR DISTRIBUTION SYSTEM

Because of the competitive price, and the rapid turnover, *Paperfronts* are possibly the most profitable line a bookseller can handle. They are stocked by the best bookshops all over the world. It may be that your bookseller has run out of stock of a particular title. If so, he can order more from us at any time—we have a fine reputation for "same day" despatch, and we supply any order, however small (even a single copy), to any bookseller who has an account with us. We prefer you to buy from your bookseller, as this reminds him of the strong underlying public demand for *Paperfronts*. Members of the public who live in remote places, or who are housebound, or whose local bookseller is unco-operative, can order direct from us by post.

FREE

If you would like an up-to-date list of all paperfront titles currently available, send a stamped self-addressed envelope to
ELLIOT RIGHT WAY BOOKS, BRIGHTON RD.,
LOWER KINGSWOOD, SURREY, U.K.